TO

_____

FROM

_____

Discovering the subtle joys *in* everyday *living*.

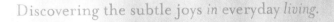

The GIFT of
small blessings

Written and compiled by
Hope Lyda

What blessing do you need?

Look for it up ahead. It awaits discovery in
your everyday life. Take your time and wander
through these blessings prepared for you and
your heart. Give yourself moments to appreciate
the blessing of breath, a brand-new day, shared
meals, kindred spirits, change, belonging, hope,
beauty, home, and so much more.

*The journey to gather blessings will turn your spirit
toward joy and your life toward gratitude.*

Let the thankful heart

SWEEP THROUGH THE DAY

and, as the magnet finds the iron,

so it will find, in every hour,

some heavenly blessings.

HENRY WARD BEECHER

Blessings surround you.

Look and you will find it—
what is unsought
will go undetected.

SOPHOCLES

When we live in a state of hurry or worry,

we can miss them,

bolt past them in the pursuit of finish lines.

But when we pay attention...

when we open our eyes to see

and our hands and hearts to receive,

the blessings are there.

Plentiful. Surprising. Brilliant.

BREATHE.

Breathe in. Breathe out.

This is your lifeline,
your source of energy
and restoration.
A measure, a grace.

*Simply being alive
is the greatest blessing
we can enjoy.*

RENE DUBOS

Your every breath
    is a reminder of
    a blessing's truest purpose...
to be drawn in fully
    and then released
    to the world
    in a new form.

May each breath you take today

fill you with gratitude

that you soon share

with another.

What could be better than a clean slate?

THIS NEW DAY

is an expanse of time and possibility

LAID OUT BEFORE YOU

like a sacred path

scrolling over unexplored hills.

May you have warm words

on a cool evening,

a full moon on a dark night,

and a smooth road

all the way to your door.

IRISH BLESSING

Set your feet firmly on today's trail.

It will lead you when you are lost.

It will reveal the hope of a destination,

even when you stumble

on the rocky terrain of doubt.

And it will always be here.

Ready. Waiting.

And promising to greet you

with everything you need.

May the promise of a new day

inspire your creativity

and unveil the way

for you to go.

What is the nudge
you have been ignoring?

Have you released your grasp
on a longheld dream?

Give yourself the blessing of change.
Even if it scares you.
Even if the loudest naysayer
is your inner voice.

DARE TO LIVE
the life you have dreamed
for yourself.
Go forward
and make your dreams
come true.

RALPH WALDO EMERSON

CHOOSE IT NOW—

that step, thought, phone call,

habit, conversation, leap,

good-bye, commitment, or prayer

that shifts you from
the "no" of status quo
to the blessing of momentum.

Blessed be your courage to change.
May today's small act
transform fear into great hope.

Scoop up well-being.
Pour kindness.
Ladle love.
Pass the peace.
So many blessings are served
when you gather round
the table with loved ones
and new acquaintances alike.

Too few of us, perhaps,
feel that breaking of bread,
the sharing of salt,
the common dipping into one bowl,
mean more than
satisfaction of a need.

We make such primal things
as casual as tunes
heard over a radio,
forgetting the mystery
and strength in both.

M. F. K. FISHER

At your next shared meal,
pause to savor the sound of laughter,
the hum of easy conversation,
and the "mmm" response
to each satisfying mouthful.
You will discover
that every part of you—
body, mind, and spirit—
is being fed.

May you seek to comfort
and be comforted each time
you nourish others
with food, love,
and friendship.

A kindred spirit

will bless your days.

They laugh with you

at life's quirkier moments.

They understand before

you fumble through explanations

of what you really meant.

And they proclaim, through words

and attentive silences, "I see you."

May your steps lead you
to a widening in the path
that makes room for two,
so you can link arms
with a kindred soul
and set out
on a brighter journey.

OH, THE COMFORT,

the inexpressible comfort
of feeling safe with a person;
having neither to weigh thoughts
nor measure words,
but to pour them all out,
just as they are,
chaff and grain together,

knowing that a faithful hand
will take and sift them,
keep what is worth keeping,
and then,
with the breath of kindness,
blow the rest away.

DINAH MARIA CRAIK

Discover the blessing
of a personal
reset button.

SWAY TO A TUNE

that restores your rhythm.
Take a moment
to thank the early bloom
or applaud the sunset

for another great show.

Learn to get in touch

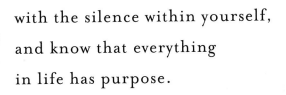

with the silence within yourself,
and know that everything
in life has purpose.

There are no mistakes, no coincidences,
all events are blessings
given to us to learn from.

ELISABETH KUBLER-ROSS

Blessed are they

who see beautiful things

in humble places

where other people see nothing.

CAMILLE PISSARRO

MAY HEALING STILLNESS

reignite your vision of possibility
and your call to live fully
and wholly as you.

Step inside...

this home,

this circle,

this embrace of a beloved.

Don't ever forget
what it feels like to be welcomed.

You belong here.

*We can only be said to be alive
in those moments
when our hearts are conscious
of our treasures.*

THORNTON WILDER

May you be known

AND HELD DEAR

ALL THE DAYS OF YOUR LIFE...

and may you always make room

for the kindness, friendship,

and wisdom encountered

along your journey.

ARE YOU IN IT...

the thick of it?

The throes of it?

Don't be guessing

if there's a blessing.

There is.

Wait for it...

*Prayers go up
and blessings come down.*

YIDDISH PROVERB

Our real blessings
often appear to us

in the shape of pains,

losses and disappointments;

but let us have patience

and we soon shall see them

in their proper figures.

JOSEPH ADDISON

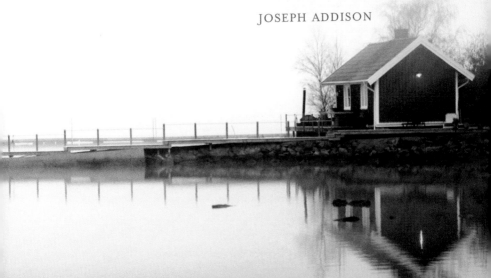

Watch for the gifts of today.
They are for your eyes to see,
your spirit to gather,
and your heart to hold.

MAY YOU BE SURPRISED

by abundance in the days ahead.

RELEASE YOUR WORRIES

so that you are free

to grab onto goodness.

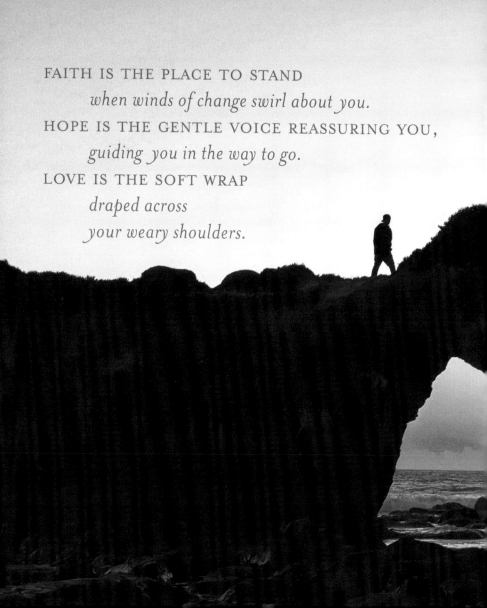

FAITH IS THE PLACE TO STAND
  when winds of change swirl about you.
HOPE IS THE GENTLE VOICE REASSURING YOU,
  guiding you in the way to go.
LOVE IS THE SOFT WRAP
  draped across
  your weary shoulders.

We look forward to the time
when the Power of Love
will replace the Love of Power.
Then will our world know
the blessings of peace.

WILLIAM GLADSTONE

Hear blessings
dropping their blossoms
around you.

RUMI

ON THE CREST OF EVERY HILL,

may you see the light

of the sun rising

to greet you on the other side

and may you hear the song

your heart

has always known.

Inspiration is

the second wind that whisks you forward.

You'll know its power when you get

the eye-opening idea at dawn

or the answer

that turns you toward hope.

WHEN WE LOSE ONE BLESSING,

*another is often most
unexpectedly given in its place.*

C.S. LEWIS

FOR FUN,

COUNT YOUR BLESSINGS

ONE BY ONE.

FOR INSPIRATION...

GO SHARE THEM WITH

SOMEONE WHO DOESN'T EXPECT

SUCH KINDNESS.

Focus on your strengths,
not your weaknesses.
Focus on your character,
not your reputation.
Focus on your blessings,
not your misfortunes.

ROY T. BENNETT

Slow down and enjoy life.

It's not only the scenery you miss

by going too fast—

you also miss the sense

of where you are going

and why.

EDDIE CANTOR

EACH YESTERDAY

has paved the way

for the possibility of now.

MAY INSPIRATION

lead to renewal today

and purpose tomorrow.

PUT THAT BURDEN DOWN.

Whatever it is,

you can tend to it later (or not).

Let yourself glide

through a day a bit lighter.

Brighter.

What might a trouble-free

Tuesday lead to?

Or a silly Saturday?

May the Great Mystery

make sunrise in your heart.

SIOUX BLESSING

DEVELOP INTEREST IN LIFE AS YOU SEE IT;

in people, things, literature, music—

the world is so rich, simply throbbing

with rich treasures,

beautiful souls and interesting people.

HENRY MILLER

As each day reveals
joy-saturated moments,

may you dive in to them.

Leave pride

and poise behind

and immerse your full being

in freedom's blessing.

Be grateful for the home you have,
knowing that at this moment,
all you have is all you need.

SARAH BAN BREATHNACH

HOME TAKES ON MANY SHAPES...

*Four walls that hold sacred space
for family and friends.*

*A person who offers
the refuge of acceptance.*

*The beating heart
that leads you back
to your longing.*

EVERYBODY CAN LOVE

in the place where they are.

WE CAN ALL

add our share of love
without leaving the room.

HELEN NEARING

May the blessing of home
give you the courage
to be present to others
with authenticity,
generosity,
and a love that transforms.

Some people come in our life
as blessings.
Some come in your life
as lessons.

MOTHER TERESA

A light heart lives long.

SHAKESPEARE

Reflect upon your present blessings—

OF WHICH EVERY MAN

HAS MANY—

not on your past misfortunes,

OF WHICH ALL MEN

HAVE SOME.

CHARLES DICKENS

I will only add, *God bless you.*

JANE AUSTEN

The Gift of Small Blessings

© 2018 KPT Publishing, LLC
Written by Hope Lyda

Published by KPT Publishing
Minneapolis, Minnesota 55406
www.KPTPublishing.com

ISBN 978-1-944833-53-4

Designed by AbelerDesign.com

First printing January 2019

10 9 8 7 6 5 4 3 2 1

Printed in the United States of America